Sweet Baby
(PEACE OF MIND)

By
LINDA CROSBY

Sweet Baby (Peace Of Mind)
Copyright © 2023 by Linda Crosby

Published in the United States of America

Library of Congress Control Number: 2024901091
ISBN   Paperback: 979-8-89091-421-7
ISBN   eBook: 979-8-89091-422-4

All rights reserved. No part of this publication may be reproduced, stored in a retrieval system or transmitted in any way by any means, electronic, mechanical, photocopy, recording or otherwise without the prior permission of the author except as provided by USA copyright law.

The opinions expressed by the author are not necessarily those of ReadersMagnet, LLC.

ReadersMagnet, LLC
10620 Treena Street, Suite 230 | San Diego, California, 92131 USA
1.619. 354. 2643 | www.readersmagnet.com

Book design copyright © 2023 by ReadersMagnet, LLC. All rights reserved.

Cover design by Ericka Obando
Interior design by Don De Guzman

Dedication

Deborah A. Quesada, MLIS, Adult Program Coordinator, she encouraged me to expand my horizon by giving me the opportunity to participate in a "Poetry Reading," at the local library.

Thank You

Roy Harrison Crosby, (AKA Sweet Baby), my husband, he is always by my side, and was my sounding board throughout the entire process of writing this book. I could not have done it without him.

Sam Diapana, ReadersMagnet, my Author Relations Officer, a Wordsmith beyond measure. This book would not be what it is without her invaluable skills.

Special Acknowledgments

All the glory belongs to God!

Mary Nell Fulton, my best friend always (BFA), of 33 plus years, she thought my work was good enough to be published, and urged me to write this book of poetry.

I *am* black, but comely, O ye daughters of Jerusalem,
as the tents of Kedar, as the curtains of Solomon.
(Song of Solomon 1:5 KJV)

Contents

Dedication .... *iii*
Thank You .... *v*
Special Acknowledgments .... *vii*
Relationships 1
Love 5
Marriage 9
Such 11
Pain 13
Friend 15
Twins 17
God 19
One Day 21
Dark Day 22
Accident 24
Sweet Baby 26
Resources and References 28

Relationships

My eyes see you, but my heart tells me to run,
Should I experience you just for fun?
Or should I dig deeper and find out you can be so much more?
I don't think so,
I'm heading for the door!

No relationship is going to be a bed of roses every day,
It does not matter what anyone say,
Remember, along with the roses come thorns,
You will be forlorn,
If the thorns become too prickly,
Run!

A broken heart can mend,
When a relationship end,
Tell it to a friend,
Hope they comprehend,
And don't condescend,
Ask for a shoulder to lend,
Don't make it a trend,
Learn from it!

In a relationship when you hear time and time again, I'm sorry,
Don't look into the eyes they are starry,
Just know it's not normal,
Don't become conformable,
Make yourself transformable,
Know, a leopard always keeps its spots!

When I took a glance,
I saw romance,
I decided to give it a chance,
Sometimes you win, sometimes you lose,
You have to play the game to sing the blues.

In a relationship when the time comes to move on, do you stay?
Try another way?
Pray, you don't regret it every day?

Some relationships can be repair,
How do you know you're not a spare?
Watch out!
Beware!

In a relationship if we say we forgive,
Why do we relive,
And blurt out dirt,
That can hurt?

In a relationship if we say we forget,
Why do we still make silly threats,
That can lead to upset,
And cause regret?

In a relationship sometimes you have to agree,
To disagree,
Turn around and flee,
To know it wasn't meant to be.

In a relationship when the trust is broken,
Sometimes, there are no words to be spoken,
It leaves you busted,
And disgusted,
Don't become combusted,
With hate,
That can lead to a worse fate.

SWEET BABY (PEACE OF MIND)

In a relationship sometimes you have to assert yourself,
To convert yourself,
To show you are not property,
Or a commodity.

In any relationship saying goodbye may be hard,
You take in regard,
What is best for you,
And you will muddle through.

Don't look into starry eyes,
They do hypnotize,
Draw you back in,
Then the craziness starts all over again!

What's with the games some people play?
Seem like they never go away,
Stop!
Be loving and kind,
And everything will work out just fine.

Relationships, Marriage, and Such,
Oh, can mean so much,
You need to take the time to let them grow,
Then you will know,
When you find out,
There is no doubt.

LINDA CROSBY

Love

Love can be beautiful if you allow it to be,
Should we spend some time together, and see?
If we decide that it's not to be,
Can we part gracefully?

Love is more than just a word,
It's a feeling that can be heard,
It's an emotion that you can see,
If you open your heart and let it be,
And it can be bittersweet,
Sometimes, it will make you weep.

Love is like a flower,
That blooms after a spring shower,
It can be tender,
Make you surrender,
If your heart gets broken,
Just chalk it up as a token.

Love is tricky,
Sometimes, can't be sticky,
You need to try and see,
If your heart can be set free.

Love can make you soar as high as the sky,
Turn around and leave you dry,
Don't cry,
At least you fly.

Love is a two-way street,

LINDA CROSBY

Be careful of the road that you take,
Sometimes it ends well,
And again, you might find yourself in hell.

What happens when you can no longer stand the person you love?
Do you still act lovey-dovey?
With all the mushy,
And gushy?
Or do you just call it a day,
And walk away?
If you do,
Don't look back!

Love can beat up on you for the last time,
Then it loses all its chime,
There's no reason for the madness,
That caused all the sadness,
Be strong!

When love is over don't feel blue,
Especially, if you did all you could do,
Just keep forging ahead,
Until you're dead.
Don't worry about would have,
Could have,
Should have,
Live!

Falling in love can be scary,
What if it makes you wary?
Should you act cherry,
When you know the situation is hairy?

To find love you get your feet wet,
To know it's a match set,
Sometimes the game is over,
Before you find your four-leaf clover.

SWEET BABY (PEACE OF MIND)

When you're in love you never could tell,
It might put you under a spell,
You can't say why,
Even if you try.

When love gets you in its grip,
You will take an amazing trip,
Watch your step,
So, you won't get prep.

Love can be a song,
That plays too long,
When the music stop,
Your heart may drop.

Life and love, a mystery,
Handed down through history,
We need to evolve,
And resolve,
The best we can,
And try to understand.

I thought my first love was my true love,
I found out I was unsure of,
It should have been a bash,
All I wanted to do was make a dash,
I did,
Now, it's just you for me kid.

Isn't it a beautiful thing to love again?
After the heartache and the pain,
Someone who's there for the sunshine and the rain,
The ups and downs,
And crazy turnarounds,
Love the second time around,
Yippee!

LINDA CROSBY

Marriage

Marriage can be a beautiful thing,
All the bling,
And wedding ring,
Behind closed door,
That's when the true feelings appear,
Pray, it's not a lawfully wedded nightmare.

Marriage is a work in progress,
What to do if it regress?
Should you try to make it a success,
Just to impress?

Marriage can be a facade,
Especially, when it's flawed,
Put on a happy face,
You can hide your disgrace.

In a marriage some people may look at self-preservation,
As being a bad thing, sometimes it depends upon the situation,
That needs to be taken into consideration,
What about annihilation?

Some people marry for financial reasons,
What about during the stormy seasons?
Do you stay for the money?
Or is it time to say goodbye, honey?

In a marriage we are one, but we are individuals,
There will be oppositional,
That comes with the transitional.

LINDA CROSBY

Such

Be careful of the people you meet,
Life is more than just a one-way street,
You should look before you advance,
Or even consider taking a chance.

When you feel drain,
Everything seems in vain,
Just remember, you can stand the rain,
And you will be yourself again.

You have to keep your faith to maintain your sanity,
To get through all of this craziness call humanity!

You have to find your place,
To feel like you're part of the human race.

Never think of yourself as less,
You're just as good as the best.

Sometimes, we have to carry on,
Despite of being forlorn,
There are always the faithful few,
Who will carry on with you,
No matter what you do.

Be thankful of the people who are there
with you through thick and thin,
You can always count on them as being written in.

I just want to be another face in the crowd,
My head is not in the cloud,
No need to stand out,
That's not what I'm all about,
I just want my time in the sun,
Before my run,
Is done.

Pain

Hey, pain,
My friend,
I wish I could say you're back again,
But you're here every day,
You never go away,
It sure would feel nice to say,
You're alright,
But you're always here, be it morning, noon, or night,
You burn me like fire,
And take away my desire,
Your numbness leaves me senseless,
And take away my defenses,
You shoot through me like a flame,
And never take the blame,
You stab me like a knife,
And cause major strife,
But you and I are in a fight to the death,
Until I take my last breath,
One day, I will be out of this tailspin,
And you will be a has-been,
I will never surrender, I will never give up,
One day, I will win the Victor's cup,
What's with the tingling,
When I'm mingling?
So, hey, pain,
My friend,
Here we go again,
Let's do this!

If people could see me inside out,
Sometimes, I just want to scream and shout,
They would know my life is so full of pain,
And may be understand,
They have no room to complain.

Friend

I have a friend closer than a father or a mother,
He is more than just a brother,
I know He cares,
He sees my tears,
He takes away all my fears,
To Him, my burdens I can share,
He is always there.

A friend like you is hard to find,
I'm so glad we are friends who can share our mind,
Friends come and go,
Our friendship continues to grow,
I just want you to know,
I treasure our friendship so,
You are my friend,
Now, and forevermore.

When you feel like you're all alone,
No one to call your own,
No worries,
You have a friend,
If you let Him in,
Need I say more?

Twins

Twins have a bond that can't be broken,
There are no words that can be spoken,
To know what twins, have in their hearts,
If they are true, they never will depart,
Such as a two of you my friends,
Always stay true to the end.

My husband is my twin,
He is closer than my kin,
I can count on him through thick and thin,
With him I will always win,
The sentiment comes from deep within.

LINDA CROSBY

God

I Pray to **God**,
In good,
In bad,
In happy,
In sad.

Pain does not care what time of day or night,
It stays with me, and I try to fight,
With all my might,
It is so hard to bear,
But I know, **God** is near.

There are days when I'm so sad and blue,
I can't see my way through,
God alone knows what to do,
I am not forgotten.

God is caring me every step of the way,
I say,
To myself, day by day,
Through Him,
I am okay.

Lying lips can take you on a trip,
If you're not careful you will slip,
Learn to take them as grains of sand,
Remember, **God** always has a plan,
If you know what I'm talking about show your hand.

You know, how you know when you're in good love?
There's no push or shove,
It's like a blessing that comes down from above,
There's no rhyme or reason,
It's just your season,
Thank **God**, for it!

Living in this world of sin and sorrow,
We sometimes, have to beg and borrow,
Be thankful, **God** always gives us tomorrow.

Sometimes, I feel like my life is just an illusion,
Wading through all the confusion,
What is the resolution?
Answer: **God**, and Prayer.

Over the years,
I have shed many tears,
I know, **God** won't put more on me, than I can bear,
I feel His presence ever near.

Life is more than just being,
You have to experience freeing,
By going out for your own wellbeing,
To see what **God** is overseeing.

One Day

One day, LORD,
No more pains,
No more sorrows,
No more tears,
No more tomorrows,
I won't be awakened because of agonizing pain,
I will be on the glory train.

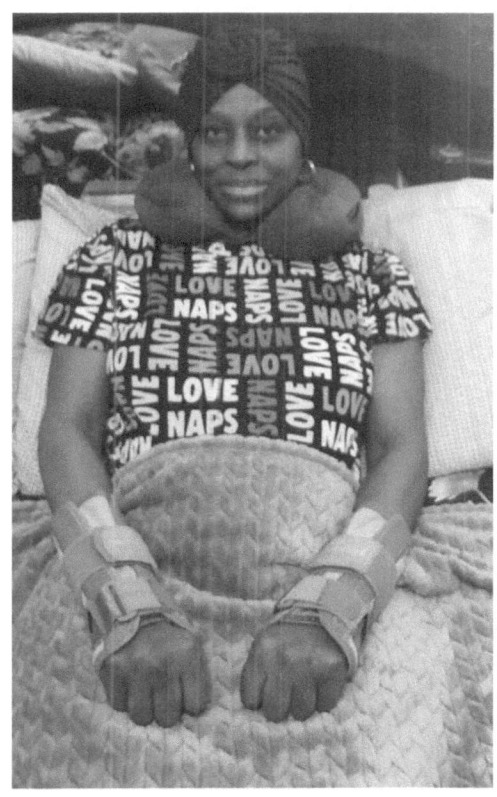

Dark Day

Sometimes, my way gets dark and dreary,
And of course, I do get weary,
But I need to get things done,
While I'm under the sun.

It is a hellacious battle,
Sometimes, I might get rattle,
But my husband is at my beck and call,
So, I will not fall.

My head is dizzy,
My mind is in a tizzy,
I feel as if I'm in a fog,
Just wanting to get out of a bog,
My brain is a backlog.

Sickness is for everyone,
Don't let it cause you to be undone,
I can barely take it anymore,
You just don't know,
But here we go.

People see me and think I'm okay,
But try to live life my way,
And you will see a day,
That you will want it to go away.

Sometimes, I wonder why I was ever born,
To be so sad and torn,
Always have to mourn,
Even get scorn,
You can run, but you cannot hide from yourself.

SWEET BABY (PEACE OF MIND)

Accident

The accident happened in two thousand one,
It ain't been no fun,
I was put into this wheelchair, in two thousand five,
But I'm still alive,
It's now, two thousand twenty-three,
So, I'm ready to be me.

The old clock on the wall,
Is saying goodbye, y'all,
Well, of course, I don't know,
But, I'm ready, for my one-woman flow.

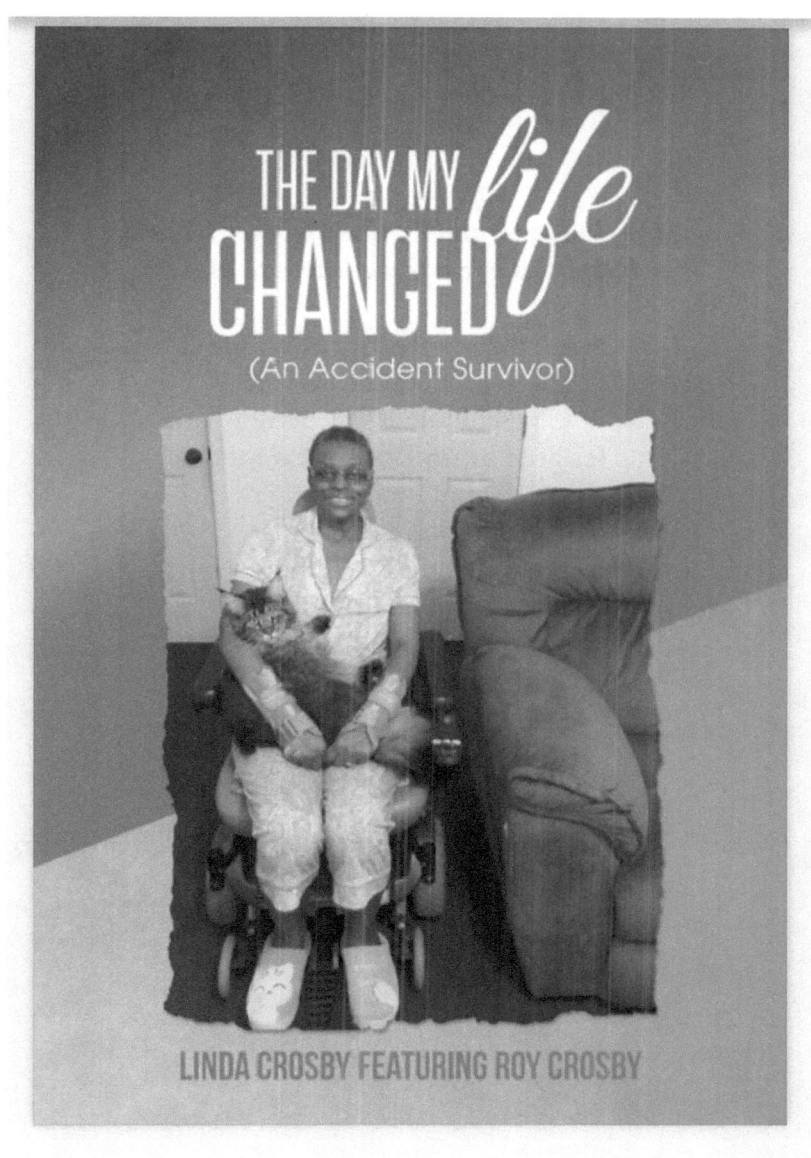

Sweet Baby

(My husband and I call each other Sweet Baby; this poem is dedicated to him.)

Sweet Baby is the love of my life,
I'm so proud to be his wife,
Life with him is lots of fun,
He's been by my side since day one,
Before I met him,
Life was a whim,
He tamed the savage beast,
Now, life is a continued feast.

My husband is a precious treasure,
He loves me beyond measure,
A rare gem that's hard to find,
Sometimes, it blows my mind,
I will never find another love like that in your lifetime or mine.
I Love You, My Sweet Baby!

SWEET BABY (PEACE OF MIND)

Resources and References

If you are interested in reading my blog, go to: *www.lindacrosbyauthor.com*.
You can purchase my Healthy Weight Loss Plan by going to my email: *lindacrosby@lindacrosbyauthor.com*.
Or on my blog and/or make a donation of your choice.
It is a secure website and all transactions are private.
If you are not comfortable putting your personal information online, please send $5, along with your email address for my Plan, and/or send a donation of your choice to P.O. Box 1084, Lake City, SC 29560. When I receive your $5, I will email my Healthy Weight Loss Plan to the address that you have provided.
Disclaimer:
Please check with your doctor before trying my Healthy Weight Loss Plan.
Even though it is personally tried and true.
What works for me, may or may not, work for you.
For more copies of Sweet Baby (Peace of Mind), go to: *www.readersmagnet.com*.
While you are there you can also find my book: The Day I Found The LORD (For Myself), and the Audiobook of my first book: The Day My Life Changed (An Accident Survivor).
To purchase my first book go to: *https://bookstore.dorrancepublishing.com/the-day-my-life-changed-an-accident-survivor/*. Or *www.dorrancebookstore.com*.
Or call Dorrance Bookstore at: 1-800-788-7654.

SWEET BABY (PEACE OF MIND)

Thank you for reading, this is Linda. ♥

www.ingramcontent.com/pod-product-compliance
Lightning Source LLC
LaVergne TN
LVHW041559070526
838199LV00046B/2057